SHUT THE LION'S MOUTH

I. B ALFA

2018

i

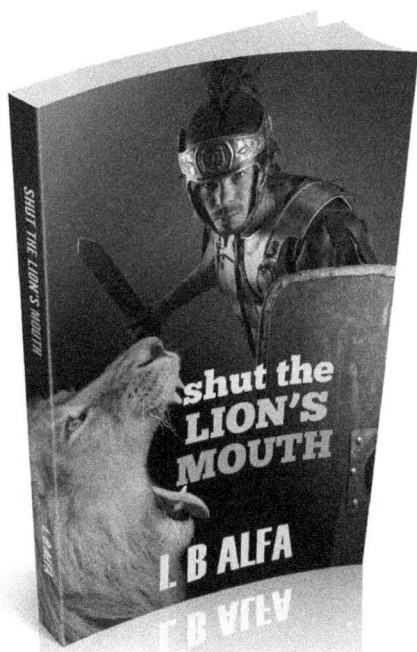

Shut The Lion's Mouth

Book Available Online
amazon.com
barnesandnoble.com
And Other Major Online Bookstores

Author's Contact
Email:alfablessing@yahoo.co.uk

Cover And Interior Design
Rehoboth House, Chicago

Printed in Lagos, Nigeria By Permission
First Print, June 2018 By Rehoboth Publishing, Lagos
Email: rehobothpublishing@gmail.com
Tel: 234 802 304 3072

Published in USA by Rehoboth House, Chicago
info@rehobothhouseonline.com
www.rehobothhouseonline.com3D COVER

REHOBOTH HOUSE

Shut The Lion's Mouth

TABLE OF CONTENTS

Shut The Lion's Mouth

DEDICATION

I dedicate this book to God the Father, God the Son, and God the Holy Spirit for divine insight and revelation in writing this book.

Shut The Lion's Mouth

AKNOWLEDGEMENT

I thank God for my wife who has never ceased to be a wonderful support to me. To Pastor Mrs Grace Alfa, I say may God honour and bless you.

To my children, thank you for being my friends and my support. God bless and keep you all.

To the Pastor in New Creation Assembly, I appreciate you all and I trust that this book will bring out the **'Lion'** in you.

I want to say thank you to Pastor Simon Ilabija for proof reading this book. You have been dutiful and may God bless you.

To the members of New Creation Assembly I bless God every day for the privilege to serve you in the Lord's vineyard and I pray that you become **'Lions'** in this end time. May you remain rapturable in Jesus name.

Sister Rahmatu Ibrahim, the ministry's media consultant has ensured a ceaseless flow in making sure my books are published. May God's mercy never cease over your life.

Finally, I appreciate the support of close relatives and friends of the ministry, including all those that will read this book. May the Lion of the tribe of Judah cause you to reign as lions in Jesus name. Amen.

INTRODUCTION

The fear of man, the government, Boko Haram in Nigeria, Al-Shabab in Kenya and Somalia, ISIS in Syria and similar terrorist groups all over the world has cast a dark shadow upon Christians. Today some churches are bare and fellowship centres empty. In fact, most Christians have compromised their faith, and some have become complacent because they want to save their lives, their jobs, their families, their marriages and even their positions and power.

The compromise in these last days in the church is alarming as unbelievers are making a mockery of our faith. These compromises have tied up the hands of God in doing signs and wonders experienced in the Bible days through the

Fathers of Faith; because they were able to withstand every form of opposition without compromise.

One typical example was Daniel. He was a slave boy captured by King Nebuchadnezzar to serve in Babylon. However, he determined in his heart never to bow to the god of Babylon by compromising his faith in the God of his fathers from the first day he was selected to undergo studies; which would qualify him to stand before the King - ***Daniel Chapter 1.***

For honouring God amongst unbelievers (Babylonians) in a strange land (Babylon) known as the ***Land of Captivity***, God proved himself amongst the Babylonians as the '**Living God**'.

Daniel through his faith in God obtained favour from King Nebuchadnezzar and Kings after King Nebuchadnezzar. He became an evangelist converting the Kings and the Kingdom to God through the awesome manifestation of God's power; because he refused to dishonor God.

He knew the God of his fathers as a mighty deliverer and his faith in God made God prove himself by shutting the lion's mouth when 120 Presidents and Princes of nations, not mere individuals, conspired against him. They knew Daniel loved God and the way they thought of getting him was through his service to God.

Knowing the consequences of his obedience to God, Daniel was not afraid. He continued serving God openly - not in hiding, and God stood for him - *Daniel Chapter 6.* He refused to save his life and God gave the lives of men for his sake.

Brethren, the manifestation of God's power today is limited compared to the times of old. This is as a result of fear and compromise amongst Christians. However, the Lord Jesus Christ says that anyone who saves his life at the expense of standing for God will lose it; but if you lose it by refusing to compromise your faith in God then you will save it - *Luke 17 v 33.*

This book will open your eyes to how much you have limited God from manifesting His power in your situation because of one compromise or the other in a bid to play safe. In fact, some tag it as wisdom, but brethren there is no wisdom in denying God. It only makes the matter worse and gives the enemy an upper hand.

There are four things in the life of Daniel which made the lions to honour him. Daniel was able to shut the mouth of ferocious lions by the power of God as a result of these four things which most Christians lack today. They will be revealed in the various chapters of this book as you read along.

The Bible refers to the devil as a roaring ferocious lion, devouring the lives of men, and Christians are no exemption because they lack the power to shut his mouth. It is my earnest prayer that after reading this book you will understand that you are a *Superior Lion* with the power to shut the mouth of lions because your father is the *Lion of the tribe of Judah,* and the son of a lion is a lion – Praise God.

God is waiting for you to take just a step for him and He will do the rest to showcase his power and might in these last days. **FEAR NOT!!!**

PASTOR I.B ALFA
The Overseer,
New Creation Assembly International.

CHAPTER 1

The Man Daniel

"And the King spake unto Ashpenaz the master of his eunuchs, that he bring certain of the children of Israel, and of the King's seeds and of the princes; children in whom was no blemish but well favoured, and skillful in all wisdom, and cunning in knowledge, and understanding science, and such as had ability to stand in the king's palace, and whom they might teach the learning and the tongue of the Chaldeans…. Now, among these were of the children of Judah, Daniel, Hananiah, Mishael, and Azariah" (Dan. 1:3 – KJV).

D aniel was not just an ordinary man. He had royal blood running through his veins. However, he was a man with exceptional characters because of his love and reverence for God; which brought him honor amongst unbelievers (Babylonians), in his land of captivity under the reign of King Nebuchadnezzar.

He was captured as a result of Israel's sins against God, which made God give them up to unbelievers as slaves. That condition was enough for anyone to feel betrayed and lost and even give up on God. It was unimaginable for someone with a royal blood to become a slave. Daniel never thought that he would one day become a slave and a captive in a strange land. The worst had hit him when it became a reality, but Daniel did not abhor God as most people would do.

He did not condition his mind to the belief that God has abandoned His people and will not show up for them in a strange land. Daniel carried God in his heart to Babylon, and refused to be corrupted by the ways and acts of the people.

Despite the fact that He was chosen to serve the King, he did not compromise his faith. He chose the will of God above comfort. He refused eating what was served to the King. Instead, he ordered to be fed with pulse (beans, lentils and peas) for three years.

Daniel from onset did not hide his identity. He made it known that bowing to the gods of Babylon was not an option for him; because he purposed in his hear to do the will of God, even as a slave despite the favour he received to serve in the palace.

> "And the king appointed them a daily provision of the king's meat, and of the wine which he drank: so nourishing them three years, that at the end thereof, they might stand before the king. But Daniel purposed in his heart that he will not defile himself with the portion of the king's meat, nor with the wine which he drank" Daniel 1 v 5 KJV).

By honouring God, God proved himself in his life and made him look and sound better than those who ate from the King's table - ***Daniel chapter 1 verse 20.*** He also obtained great favour before the King.

Daniel in all of these never gave himself glory but always showcased God as a great God. He made the Kings to realize that his God is the Almighty, and this in turn made them to honour Daniel's God.

From the days of King Nebuchadnezzar when the King was tormented by his dream and sought for the man who will reveal the dream and the meaning, Daniel gave glory to God for this ability.

> *"But there is a God in heaven that revealeth secrets, and maketh known to the king Nebuchadnezzar what shall be in the latter days" (Daniel 2:28 - KJV).*

> *"The king answered unto Daniel and said, Of a truth it is, that your God is a God of gods, and a Lord of kings, and a revealer of secrets, seeing thou couldest reveal this secret" (Daniel 2:47 – KJV).*

The only reason King Nebuchadnezzar gave glory to the God of Daniel was because Daniel never failed to reverence God. Unlike these days when Christians are quick to give themselves and men glory and honour due to God. Some ministers are also in this category, that is why you see some of them who reigned in time past have faded away. However, Daniel's fame and greatness continued even after King Nebuchadnezzar to King Belshazzar and to the reigns of King Darius and King Cyrus.

Daniel was not a selfish man. He was not self-seeking, but he thought of the wellbeing of his fellow brothers. A character trait which is exceptional. Today, people are scared of introducing their fellow brethren to their benefactors so that they will not be betrayed, or ousted from their positions by their brethren. There is no genuine love and trust. Some just want to be the only ones prospering so that others will look up to them, serve them and beg from them. However, Daniel wanted Shedrach, Meshach and Abednego, his Hebrew brothers to be well placed in Babylon - *Daniel 2 v 49.*

Daniel was steadfast with God in the face of opposition and conspiracy. He was not afraid of the consequences of his being steadfast with God in disobedience to the laws of the land. He was the only one in the Bible that co – habited with lions, and came out from their den alive - *Daniel Chapter 6.*

Daniel's loyalty to God at the expense of the laws of the Kings of Babylon made God to work wonders for him, and this humbled the Kings. Because of this man, psalms were made by King Nebuchadnezzar and King Darius about the might and power of the God of Daniel, and decrees to worship Daniel's God referred to as the **'Living God'** were established.

Just one man was able to do this in a whole Kingdom. He came in as a slave and became an authority taking the whole land of Babylon for God. How many Christians can do that today? How many are willing to go out of their comfort zones to mission fields? How many are willing to say if I perish I perish and damn the consequences?

This is the reason we hardly hear awesome testimonies of Gods saving grace like in the days of Daniel. God is looking for men like Daniel in our time to show forth His mighty works in the affairs of men.

The Land of Captivity

Babylon was a land of captivity for the children of Israel. God used Babylon to punish them as a result of their disobedience. Today, it is found in the present day Iraq and was known for its idolatry and sin.

During the reign of King Hezekiah, when envoys from Babylon came to Jerusalem - *2 Kings 20 v 12 – 19*, Prophet Isaiah chastised the King for showing out the treasures of Judah to them, and predicted that Babylon will one day carry these riches off. This was a startling revelation because Assyria was the great power of the day and seemingly assailable. However, the continuous rebellion of the children of Israe; made God to hand them over to the Babylonians as slaves.

Today, Christians all over the world are under the yoke of Babylon which are represented by: evil government policies, demonic bosses, unfriendly friends, evil spouses, bad relatives, terrorist groups and even harsh economies etc. These unpleasant situations bedeviling believers is similar to what the Israelites faced in their land of captivity.

When disobedience creeps into your relationship with God, God allows you to face Babylon, with the hope that you will repent and return to Him in all sincerity and forsake your sins. However, some people blame the situation and forget to search themselves to know why they are in that predicament. By so doing, they cannot be restored from their Babylon.

A similar situation is what is happening in Nigeria. The fear of Boko Haram, Fulani Herdsmen, Militants, Unfavourable government policies and Lack of government protection, can be seen as the Babylon bedeviling Christians which has stolen their boldness and willpower in serving God genuinely; as most of them are in compromised situations in a bid to stay alive. All the same, God needs a Daniel to stand up and confront these evils so that He can showcase His might as the '**Living God**' in Nigeria.

Whatever your Babylon is that has kept you in bondage as a result of one reason or the other, today receive the boldness to declare Jesus above that Babylon and be free in Jesus name.

CHAPTER 2

The Evil Conspiracy

"Many are the afflictions of the righteous: but the LORD delivereth him out of them all" (Psalm 34:19KJV).

Conspiracies are bound to occur in the life of a Christian and a non-Christian; however the saving grace for believers to overcome is based on their relationship with God. He must be right standing with God (righteous) in order to remain victorious.

Conspiracies occur when people realize that you are favoured above them in every way. When they begin to oppose you, know clearly that they are after your position and the blessings you have received or are due to receive.

Conspirators can go to any length in making sure that they get rid of you no matter what it would cost them as seen in the book of *Daniel chapter 6.* The King preferred Daniel above all the 120 princes and the 3 presidents he set over Babylon. Daniel was the number 1 amongst them, because he had an excellent spirit.

His track record from the days of King Nebuchadnezzar and King Belshazzar were spotless – no case of tyranny, embezzlement, fraud, or ungodliness. He had a clean record which King Darius must have heard about and seen. His promotion caused envy amongst the princes and presidents in the entire kingdom.

This goes to show that every leader knows who deserves promotion or not. They know the character of those under them as there are track records to prove it. Therefore, learn to serve well in order to enjoy favour and promotion, and stop rivaling your leaders.

Daniel was not just a stranger but a slave boy who came to rule and dominate in a strange land. This did not only cause envy but hatred as they sought for his life. He was a righteous man and the only way his conspirators could trap him was through his service to God.

I am certain that his conspirators were one time friends of

his, but as soon as they noticed that Daniel was leaving them behind, and waxing stronger and greater than them, their envy became ruthless and the only thing they were after was to get him rid of him.

It is advisable that when God begins to lift you above those you were in the same level with or above those who were giving you alms to live on, then you must learn to separate yourself from them so that your relationship will not get sour. If you don not separate from them, for no just cause you will notice that they will begin to show you negative attitudes or unnecessarily criticize you, because they are not happy that you have left them behind.

Jacob was wise when he left Laban at the time that he did because his wealth had surpassed that of Laban which put his life and family at risk - *Genesis 31 V 1 & 22.* Do not be afraid of progress when God lifts you because He that lifts you has the power to protect you and all that concerns you. In psychology it is said that: '*It is better to be shown jealousy than pity*".

> "*Then said these men, We shall not find any occasion against this Daniel, except we find it against him concerning the law of his God". All the presidents of the kingdom, the governors, and the princes, the counselors,*

and the captains, have consulted together to establish a royal statute, and to make a firm decree, that whosoever shall ask a petition of any God or man for thirty days, save of thee, O king, he shall be cast into the den of lions. Wherefore King Darius signed the writing and the decree" (Daniel 6 v 5, 7, 9 KJV).

Daniel was not afraid of the well thought out conspiracy against him. He witnessed the conspiracy against Shadrach, Meshach and Abednego in **Daniel Chapter 3,** and he was confident that the God who divided the red sea, and slew the Egyptians, who wroth great wonders before he was born and who made him great in a strange land amongst other Jews and Babylonians will rise up to deliver him. Daniel knew his God.

Daniel continued serving God after he heard what had happened. He did not go into hiding as most Christians today would do; neither did he compromise his faith, knowing that his disobedience to the law equals death. He stood his ground for God to show up.

His conspirators found him praying to God and so they did not waste any time in reporting Daniel to the King. They were glad that their plan to trap him was successful. The Bible made us understand that they pressured the king against Daniel to do their bidding according to the law – Daniel Chapter 6 v 15.

They did not regard Daniel as a President. In fact to them he was still a slave. They referred to him as: *"That Daniel which is of the children of the captivity of Judah" - Daniel 6 v 13*. They did not show any regard for Daniel before the King who installed him as a President. To them he was a mere slave boy who came to dominate them in their land. That was the extent of their hatred for him.

It does not matter if you are in a disadvantaged position. It does not even matter if people look down on you. Never you look down on yourself but trust God to lift you up. If God can lift Daniel who had the tag of a slave boy on his face; then your lifting has nothing to do with your language, colour, height, looks, family background, education and status, or what anyone says about you. God will lift you up, only hold on to Him.

The King was sad and was not happy for signing the law as seen in *Daniel 6*. He loved Daniel so much that he felt sad about the whole event. The King was not a Jew which confirms scriptures that when a man pleases God, God will in turn make his enemies to be at peace with him - *Proverbs 15 v 17*. That was the scenario between the King and Daniel.

Babylonians, Medes and Persians were no friends of Jews, but Daniels case was different. He was loved by the King, because he was righteous and God fearing. A quality which is very rare amongst Christians of today.

The King summoned Daniel with a heavy heart, and threw him into the den of lions. He was not just thrown into the den, ***verse 17 of Daniel chapter 6*** made us understand that a stone was brought and laid upon the mouth of the den so that he would not escape, or none would save him. They went further to ensure that the King sealed the stone with his signet and with the signet of the Lords so that the judgment might not be changed against Daniel.

I do not know who has concluded any conspiracy against you. I do not know who has said you will never get out of the challenge you are going through, I do not know who has said you will never see help or you will never rise above this level but as long as the God that delivered Daniel is still alive every evil conspiracy and judgments against you is dissolved today by the power in the name of Jesus Christ. Amen!!!

Daniel was not thrown into a bird's cage or a dog's kennel. He was thrown into the den of lions which shows that there was more than one lion. There is no way that anyone can survive being in the captivity of ferocious carnivorous animals like lions. A lion is the strongest of all the animals and is referred to as the ***King of the Jungle***. No animal dares contend with a lion. It does not eat anything killed and offered to it. It prefers to kill its prey and eat it fresh as it is. A lion is always on an attack mode; ready to devour.

It was in the company of this animal that Daniel was thrown into. However, while Daniel's conspirators went home satisfied that the deed had been done and no reversal, the King was dying in silence. He could not sleep. He knew he had made a wrong decision but he was helpless. The King allowed himself to be flattered by the princes decided to eulogize him as a god with his own consent just for 30days. This decision eventually cost him his sleep and his joy.

The conspiracy against Daniel was also indirectly against the King. They knew the decision that the King took will hurt him and for them it served him right for honouring a slave above them. This is reflected in the way they addressed Daniel before the King. They referred to Daniel as "That Daniel" and "a slave boy" - Daniel 6 v 13, before the King's face without any regard for the King or Daniel.

It is vital that leaders must not allow themselves to be flattered or allow themselves play god in people's lives. We must be careful and watchful against flatteries which could lead to making the wrong decisions. Leaders must be bold enough to stand for the truth by discerning the intentions of counsels from those under them so that they will not make wrong decisions.

"Then the king went to his palace, and passed the night fasting: neither were instruments of musick brought

before him: and his sleep went from him. Then the king arose very early in the morning, and went in haste unto the den of lions. And when he came to the den, he cried with a lamentable voice unto Daniel: and the king spake and said to Daniel, O Daniel, servant of the living God, is thy God, whom thou servest continually, able to deliver thee from the lions?" (Daniel 6 v 18 – 20 KJV).

In the above passage we see that the King became sorrowfully burdened and fasted for Daniel. He trusted that the God of Daniel would deliver Daniel as seen in his statement in **Daniel 6 verse 16** "Thy **God whom thou servest continually, he will deliver thee.**" Despite the King's worry, Daniel was having a good time in the lion's den. Halleluyah!

I am sure Daniel was elated by the raw miraculous power of deliverance from God. He was basked in the euphoria of worship to God, because he was a man that enjoyed the presence of God.

Daniel calmed the fears of the King and still gave honour to a man who decided to throw him into the lion's den to be devoured by saying: *"O King, live forever"* - *Daniel 6 v* **21.** This exemplary character of humility was one reason I am definite that the King loved Daniel so much; because he knew how to give honour to whom honour is due even in difficult situations.

Learn to give honour to whom honour is due so that you will continually find favour. Christianity does not mean that you should be unruly even in the face of standing up for the truth. It is important that you show love, respect and honour to those in authority and people you come across with even when they do not treat you well.

Daniel went further and told the King that God sent his angel to shut the mouth of the lions and no manner of hurt was done to him The King was exceedingly glad. Immediately, the King ordered that Daniel be brought up out of the lion's den and was inspected to ascertain if truly there was no hurt or scratch on Daniel - *Daniel 6 v 22 & 23.*

The King wasted no time in casting not only Daniel's accusers but their families, and entire generations into the lion's den to be devoured. God also wasted no time in releasing the mouth of the lions to devour them. In fact, the speed at which the lions devoured them was unusual as they did not allow them to land into the den. The lions jumped at their prey in the air and consumed them - *Daniel 6 v 24.*

God will not sit still and watch your enemies rubbish you as a result of your obedience and relationship with Him. The mistake Daniel's conspirators made was to trap him through his loyalty to God. God turned the trap against them, and all that concerns them because He is jealous over His own and will not allow them to be destroyed. The church of Jesus Christ is built by Christ and the gates of hell shall not prevail against it - *Mathew 16 v 18.*

I prophesy concerning you reading this book that in the mighty name of Jesus Christ, God will completely wipe out every power and strongman that has dug your grave, and is waiting patiently for your demise. They will go for you in a hurry, that there shall be no trace of them and all connected to them that might arise to threaten your peace and steal your joy. Amen!

Daniel became the evangelist of his time. The awesome wonder of God led to a decree in the entire Kingdom which rubbished all other gods of the land, as the King himself who was not a Jew, but an unbeliever made a decree that only the God of Daniel should be served and worshipped.

> *"Then King Darius wrote unto all people, nations, and languages, that dwell in all the earth; Peace be multiplied unto you. I make a decree, That in every dominion of my kingdom men tremble and fear before the God of Daniel: for he is the living God, and steadfast forever, and his kingdom that which shall not be destroyed, and his dominion shall be even unto the end. He delivereth and rescueth, and he worketh signs and wonders in heavens and in the earth, who hath*

delivered Daniel from the power of the lions" (Daniel 6:25 – 28 - KJV).

Can you imagine an unbeliever composing a psalm to the God of Daniel because of one man who refused to compromise but he believed in the saving power of his God. Today, we pray for the salvation of souls, and also pray for God's saving grace upon our dear nations; however God will not come down to do it. He needs you and I to stand up and declare his name and Lordship in the midst of the storm so that He can prove his name as *The Living God*, which will draw men and our nations to him.

Now what is the secret of Daniel's power? How did he shut the lion's mouth? You will find the answers in the next four chapters. I pray for you that God will empower you to shut the mouth of every lion in your life in Jesus name. Amen.

The Power Of Faith

Faith is a must have for every believer who certainly wants to make heaven. Everything positive in life only comes by faith including relating with God whom you have not seen; as the Lord Jesus Christ told Thomas "... *blessed are they that have not seen, and yet have believed" (John 20 v29).*

In theology another word for faith is *'Believism'.* Having complete assurance and trust in God is what qualifies your faith in Him as the master and keeper of your today, your tomorrow and your future. The Bible defines faith thus:

"Now faith is the substance of things hoped for, the evidence of things not seen" (Hebrews 11:1 - KJV).

"Faith is the confidence that what we hope for will actually happen; it gives us assurance about things we cannot see" (New Living Translation (NLT)

Daniel had confidence that God who made him a ruler in a strange land will never forsake him. His faith in God moved God to defend His name as Daniel's God. He was able to see the raw demonstration of God's power in the shadow of death when his doom was sealed; but God rewrote his story and sealed the doom of his conspirators.

"So Daniel was taken up out of the den, and no manner of hurt was found upon him, because he believed in his God" (Daniel 6 v 23b - KJV).

Daniel's faith pleased God so much that God had to show up. The above scripture makes us to understand that one key reason the lions could not harm Daniel was because Daniel had faith in God. He believed God. Hallelujah!

He did not just believe in God when he saw that his end had come or because he was in trouble as most Christians do. They turn to God fasting and praying for exams, jobs, travel visas, marriage, ill health and the list goes on, and then forget God when they have gotten their request. Daniel had a lifestyle of believing God from the first day he was selected to stand before the king.

In Biblical theology, Daniel's *'Believism'* came from these two words:

Belief in God – The Bible makes it clear that: *"without faith it is impossible to please God, and anyone who comes to God must believe that He is"* - *Hebrews 11 v 6* – meaning He is who He says He is just as He told Moses – *"I AM THAT I AM"*. He is not lesser than who He is. He is God the Almighty and He exists. Daniel believed that the God of his father does exist and there is no variableness to Him. This was exhibited in his prayer life – *Daniel 6 v 10 & 11.*

Belief in God's Power – Daniel solely believed in the power of his God. He consulted God on every occasion even in times of trouble right from the days of King Nebuchadnezzar to King Belshazzar, to King Darius and King Cyrus. The Kings in turn believed God because of Daniel's belief in the power of God to reveal mysteries and to do wonders. Through his belief in God he was able to win the whole of Babylon to the worship and reverence of the only *'Living God'* because no other god could demonstrate raw powers like the God of Daniel.

Daniel's faith in God led him to sacrifice his life for God as Abraham was ready to sacrifice his only son to God. God blessed Abraham and saved the life of his son, and God did same for Daniel and made Daniel great in Babylon.

Today, Daniel's name is amongst the names on the biblical hall of fame in *Hebrews 11 v 32 & 33*. No other person in the Bible could break Daniel's record of shutting the mouth of lions as it became his insignia to date. He trusted God enough to put all his eggs in God's basket which did not break as opposed to the wisdom of the world which says: *"do not put all your eggs in one basket"*. Many pastors today are sharing their eggs in God's basket and the basket of Satan through fraud, charms and idolatry.

What you believe is your power. Daniel's power to rise above all situations was his belief in God. This placed him as head of all the province of Babylon and chief of all the governors of the wise men including the magicians and astrologers – *Daniel 2 v 48*. He was physically and spiritually above powers of darkness because of his unshaking belief in God. There is nothing you lose for God that you do not gain back in a million fold. Just have faith.

Martin Luther King Jnr says: *"Faith is taking the first step even when you don't see the whole staircase"*

While Evangelist Billy Graham of blessed memory rounds it up by stating and I quote:

> *"The greatest legacy one can pass to one's children and grandchildren is not money and other material things*

accumulated in one's life, but rather a legacy of character and faith".

Shut The Lion's Mouth

CHAPTER 4

The Power Of Righteous Living

"But seek ye first the kingdom of God and his righteousness; and all these things shall be added to you" *(Mathew 6 v 33 KJV).*

Many Christians today are fond of *'seeking the kingdom'*. Churches are filled with people seeking the kingdom for wealth, protection, marriage, children, miracles, signs and wonders. Some are very dutiful in doing kingdom work. You find them in the ushering department, choir department, evangelism department, even in the pastorate.

They seek the kingdom, and do the kingdom work without righteousness that is why you hear horrible sinful stories about ministers, workers even church members which should not be the case as is prevalent today.

Without righteousness which is synonymous with holiness you cannot see God - *Hebrews 12 v 14,* because God is Holy and He wants you to be in right standing with him. You cannot be a compromising Christian and be right standing with God. You must be righteous.

> *"My God hath sent his angel, and hath shut the lions' mouths, that they have not hurt me; forasmuch as before him innocency was found in me; and also before thee, O king, have I done no hurt"(Daniel 6 v 22 – KJV).*

The above scripture can be rephrased as: ***"righteousness, holiness, purity, faithfulness was found in me"***. Daniel made the King understand that it takes a man to be righteous before he can draw the mighty hand of God to fight for him, because God abhors sinners.

Daniel made it known that he is blameless before God who he firstly made obeisance to, followed by the king. His reverence to God was unparalleled and he never hesitated in making it known to the Kings he served.

As a trained theologian, I studied demonology as a course and realised that even forces of darkness cannot afflict anyone without finding out the person's offence. They must examine a person before passing judgement, because there are some people they must never touch or they risk their destruction.

I watched a converted witch saying on Daystar Channel (Joni Lamb's Talk Programme) on DSTV Cable Network that it is dangerous for a witch to curse a Christian because it must definitely backfire. She was not talking about nominal Christians who do not even read their Bible, She was referring to Christians who are in right standing before God.

> *"Then the presidents and princes sought to find occasion against Daniel concerning the kingdom; but they could find none occasion nor fault; forasmuch as he was faithful, neither was there any error or fault found in him" (Daniel 6 v 4 - KJV).*

His conspirators looked for where he had erred in matters concerning the kingdom; they found none. They did not relent as they checked where he could be faulted concerning other matters both public and private matters outside his office affairs, they still could not find any. He was faultless, because righteousness spoke for him.

It is not a surprise that they were envious of him. The Bible says it all that every other thing that makes you outstanding above your peers, your classmates, your colleagues, your family members, your relatives and even your friends would be added unto you if you seek the kingdom and attach righteousness to it - meaning being completely *'Christlike'* in every area.

When no fault can be found in you and concerning the way you conduct yourself, and your office then you are a person one can trust. That is called *'Fidelity'*. There are people who cannot be trusted with any responsibility at all, because they lack fidelity.

I met a very rich man who told me of one of his staff. He said all his wealth is in the hands of his staff. I was amazed. He did not say all his wealth is in the hands of his wife, his children or his relatives. He said a staff, a complete stranger. He stated further that for over 10 years this trusted staff of his has been working and living with him, and he has never stolen a dime.

When you are righteous, you will abhor anything that will tarnish your personality. The Bible says: *"A good name is rather to be chosen than great riches..." Proverbs 22v1 (KJV)*. A righteous man avoids anything that will give him a bad reputation, so that he can be trusted.

In the 60's in Nigeria, Christians were given loans without collateral because they were considered to be faithful. This continued even into the 70's. They were preferred to be given jobs rather than non-Christians because of what they were known to stand for which is righteousness. Today, people are careful when dealing with Christians because they have been corrupted by the standards of the world, and very few are right standing with God, and faithful in their dealings.

The letters to the various churches in the book of Revelation shows the era of the church. Today, we are in the era of the church of Laodicea where the church is lukewarm but very rich. However, God sees the church as wretched, miserable, poor, blind and naked *(Revelations 3 v14 – 22)*. God is warning the church to rise up in righteousness and zealousness, and repent in order to overcome.

The other day I saw in the Nigerian national newspapers, a Pastor showing off a car he bought for N40, 000,000:00 (Forty Million Naira). Another Pastor in Abuja, Nigeria came up and showcased his car he bought for N30,000,000:00 (Thirty Million Naira). In fact I was just amazed at the show of carnality and poverty of the word in the church today. The miserable thing is that the members are struggling to survive while the disparity between the shepherd and the sheep is widening on a daily basis.

No wonder the church which is known to be the first Non-Government Organisation (NGO) in the world; poised with the assignment of meeting the needs of the poor and needy as seen with the early disciples, has been subjected to paying taxes in Nigeria because some churches are wealthier than some government parastatals.

Many Christians are running after all other things and not the kingdom in righteousness, holiness and the fear of God. They have turned the church to a circus *"the more you look the less you see"*. They come to be entertained with dramatic expressions of pastors in casting out demons, healing the sick, and showing how anointed they are as they have mixed Christianity with mysticism in order to deceive and milk the flock.

> *"Nevertheless, the foundation of Christ standeth sure, having this seal, The Lord knoweth them that are his. And, Let everyone that nameth the name of Christ depart from iniquity" (2 Timothy 2 v 19 - KJV).*

Joseph understood that the only way he could survive in Egypt, was to depart from iniquity, and as he stood in righteousness all other things were added unto him. Mordecai stood for righteousness in a strange land, and all other things were added unto him. Jacob told Laban that his righteousness will speak for him and he became wealthier than Laban – all other things were added unto him. Daniel, Shadrach, Meshach, and Abednego stood for righteousness and all other things were added unto them.

It is important to note that Daniel, Shadrach, Meshach and Abednego were not the only Jews selected to learn the ways of the Babylonians but they were recorded as righteous refusing to defile themselves while nothing was heard about the other Jews.

There is a difference between a Christian who stands in righteousness and a carnal Christian. The reason we see Christians enduring poverty, disease and lack is because they are neither hot nor cold. They accept whatever comes their way as long as it is the norm, and they are too reluctant to go the extra mile for God in standing out as righteous so that they will not be branded as 'fanatics', 'over sabi', 'too know' or 'S.U' (Scripture Union).

> *"Thou lovest righteousness, and hated wickedness: therefore God, thy God, hath anointed thee with the oil of gladness above thy fellows" (Psalm 45 v 7 - KJV).*

Only righteousness makes you stand out from the pack. Only righteousness guarantees prosperity. Stop envying unbelievers who are doing better than you because their end is destruction – *(Psalm 37)*.

God cannot move in the midst of a perverse generation where the church has been turned to an entertainment centre and the messages on holiness and righteousness and the fear of God forsaken.

Keep on serving God in righteousness and you will definitely tell the story. If Daniel's conspirators with all their affluence, Haman with all his affluence, Herod with all his affluence, King Ahab with all his affluence could end up in destruction, I assure you that same applies to the unrighteous, but the righteous will be exalted.

The devil could not lay a charge on the Lord Jesus Christ as much as he tried. Satan found nothing to hold against Jesus, and like Daniel's conspirators the Devil used the righteousness of Christ as a charge against Him which ultimately led to the Lord Jesus being exalted as the *'Lord of lords'* and the *'King of Kings'*.

Just like Daniel, anyone who digs a pit for you because of your service to God will end up in that same pit. Jesus rose from the pit the devil dug for Him. He took the authority of Satan over death and hell, and became the head of principalities, and is exalted above every other name. Praise God!

CHAPTER 5

The Power Of Steadfastness

Steadfastness in your relationship with God proves your love for God; which helps in stimulating growth in your Christian faith. A Christian who is not steadfast with God cannot hear from God. God will be far from such a person and will not trust him with kingdom secrets and revelations.

The Cambridge dictionary defines being steadfast as: *"staying the same for a long time and not changing quickly or unexpectedly"*. Synonyms for being steadfast include being *firm, resolute, consistent, fixed* and *determined*. Therefore, being steadfast means *"being resolute or dutifully firm and unwavering to someone, something or a cause"*.

> *"Therefore, my beloved brethren, be ye steadfast, unmovable, always abounding in the work of the Lord" (1 Corinthians 15 v 58 – KJV).*

Steadfastness or being resolute or firm is an essential Christian character. It means cleaving to God. It is your ability to trust, rest, and abide in Christ no matter what the raging storms of life brings. A Christian cannot be referred to as a *'Victorious Christian'* when this character is wanting.

Daniel did not waiver in his relationship with God, neither was he hypocritical about his service to God. He was in continuous service with God every day of his life in Babylon. He had his quiet moments communing with God three times in a day and he never missed it for a single day.

His conspirators knew his schedule which made it easy for them to trap him while praying. He enjoyed God and cherished his relationship with Him. He was known to be steadfast with God even by the Kings of Babylon.

> *"Then the King commanded, and they brought Daniel, and cast him into the den of lions. Now the king spake and said unto Daniel, Thy God whom thou servest continually, he will deliver thee" (Daniel 6 v 16 – KJV).*

King Darius knew that Daniel served God continually. He believed that for Daniel to exact so much energy in serving God, then there must be something about Daniel's God that is not found in other gods. This he found out when Daniel came out from the lion's den alive! The King made a decree, declaring God's steadfastness in delivering those who trust in Him.

> *"I make a decree that in every dominion of my kingdom men tremble and fear before the God of Daniel; for he is the living God, and steadfast forever" (Daniel 6:26 - KJV).*

Before Daniel's experience in the lion's den, King Nebuchadnezzar also composed psalms to the God of Daniel – *Daniel 2 v 47, Daniel 4 v 34 – 37.* God showcased his power in saving Daniel from the lion's den because he never denied God even in trouble. He refused to abandon his relationship with God and continued steadfastly despite the fact that his life was at stake.

Apostle Paul like Daniel had suffered so much which he believed was not enough to separate him from the love of God - *Romans 8 v 31 – 39.* He suffered shipwreck, imprisonment, hunger, abuse, abandonment, yet he stood to the end, enduring the persecutions and looking unto Jesus Christ, the author and finisher of his faith.

You have a duty as a Christian to be steadfast in your relationship with God. You must not be led by your feelings or by what the majority are doing. You must be led by the

Spirit of God in all matters even if it is not in line with the majority view.

The only way you can resist the devil and make him flee from you is when you are steadfast, unmovable and unshakeable in your relationship with God. Jesus Christ reached his goal and fulfilled his assignment despite the temptations, tests and trials from man and the devil because he was steadfast.

> *"Blessed is the man who remains steadfast under trial, for when he has stood the test he will receive the crown of life, which God has promised to those who love him"* *(James 1 v 12 – KJV).*

The attack on Christians today from the home front, the society and from the government has cast a dark shadow on Christians who prefer to save their lives at the expense of losing it. In the North and Middle Belt regions of Nigeria, the fear of terrorist groups, from Boko Haram to the Fulani Jihadists have made many abandon their worship centres. Many are no longer steadfast in their attendance to Church services and other Church programmes.

Christians in Nigeria are not the only ones going through this persecution. All over the world the persecution of Christians is becoming the order of the day and the love of many are waxing cold just as the scriptures predicted – ***Mathew 24 v 12.***

Boldness to be steadfast for God in any situation be it good or bad is what will move the Mighty Hand of God to fight for you. God cannot defend someone who is neither hot nor cold. He cannot even defend anyone who is cold. You need to be hot for Him in order to experience His salvation.

The desire for miracles, signs and wonders have made many ministers and members to seek powers from the Kingdom of darkness. Many church altars are erected upon the altar from hell where members are being deceived and initiated without even knowing it because they lack the word.

Today the show of pride, lust and desperate desire for wealth has divided the hearts of Pastors from being consistent with God. They have imbibed the world's standards forsaking Gods standard in the name of applying wisdom just for the sake of their bellies.

Shut The Lion's Mouth

CHAPTER 6

The Power Of Prayer

"To be a Christian without prayer is no more possible than to be alive without breathing"
MARTIN LUTHER.

Prayer simply put is talking with God. It is the greatest of all the attributes a Christian should have in order to live a *Victorious Christian Life*. It is a communication process that allows us to talk with God.

God wants us to communicate with him as we do with one another – that is it should be spontaneous and not restricted to a certain stereotyped period of time (morning and evening). He wants us to speak to him as regular as we make phone calls, because He uses prayer to communicate with us.

It is obvious that when we do not know how to communicate with one another we will end up having misunderstandings. Problems in any kind of relationship are mostly caused by lack of communication. It is the same with God. We cannot have a good relationship with God if we do not know how to communicate with Him.

The Bible makes us understand that God is Spirit and approaching God in prayer should be done in *Spirit* and in *Truth*. That is why for the Christian, prayer is not a mere exercise it is a spiritual exercise that involves the attention of God the Father, God the Son, and God the Holy Spirit.

> *"True prayer is neither a mere mental exercise nor a vocal performance. It is far deeper than that – it is spiritual transaction with the creator of Heaven and Earth"*
> *CHARLES SPURGEON*

We pray to the Father, through the Son and with the help of the Holy Spirit who helps us to pray in wordless groaning because we do not know how to pray – *Romans 8 v 26*. The Bible says none can go to God except through Christ so all prayers and supplications are done and answered in the name that is above every other name – *JESUS (John 14 v 6, Philippians 2 v9)*

The only thing that the devil cannot do is to pray. He can sing, prophesy, preach, quote the scriptures and pretend to be a sheep but his damnation has made him an abomination to God that he dares not pray. The devil is afraid of the Christian who knows how to pray.

In spiritual theology, prayer is the major evidence of your spiritual life, and lack of prayer is an evidence of your carnality. A prayerful Christian is a victorious Christian. It is in prayer that spiritual wars which control the physical are fought and won. A Christian who does not know how to pray will live a manipulated and oppressed life. He will be a pawn in the hands of the devil.

> *"One of those days, Jesus went out to a mountain side to pray, and spent the night praying to God"(Luke 6:12 - KJV).*

> *"Watch and pray so that you will not fall into temptation. The spirit is willing, but the flesh is weak"(Mathew 26:41 - KJV).*

The Lord Jesus Christ was a man that was given to much prayer. Even as God in the form of man, he demonstrated humility by praying to the Father in order to ensure connectivity. He drew strength from prayers and prayed even to His last breath.

He knew very well the weaknesses and challenges of the flesh that was why he had a rigorously praying ministry which extended even to the night. If the Lord Jesus Christ could do vigils then it is important that we as Christians ought to follow this order in a bid to overcome.

When the challenges of the flesh came mightily upon the Lord Jesus Christ at the *Garden of Gethsemane*, he took it to God in prayer. At the *Garden of Gethsemane*, He did not only ask for strength in completing His assignment but also reversed the curse placed on man at the *Garden of Eden* through prayer.

In *Genesis Chapter 3 v 17*, God cursed the ground as a result of man's sins at the *Garden of Eden*, Jesus Christ at the end of his ministry went to the *Garden of Gethsemane* which is symbolic to Eden and reversed the curse on man through his tears of blood. The Garden was the first place that His blood was shed. As they fell to the ground, the curse was reversed because it only takes God to reverse a curse placed by God; as His tears of blood served as atonement before the final atonement on the cross.

The coming of our Lord Jesus Christ was to redeem man completely from the curse of sin and of the law which was crowned by His death on the cross. It was a curse to die on the cross; however He became a curse for us so that you and I can live a curse free victorious life in Him – *Galatians 3 v 13*.

"Now when Daniel knew that the writing was signed, he went into his house; and his windows being open in his chamber toward Jerusalem. He kneeled upon his knees three times a day, and prayed, and gave thanks before his God, as he did aforetime" (Daniel 6 v 10 – KJV).

Daniel was a man that was given to prayer. His prayer life was exceptional. He had an attitude of praying thrice a day. He was also a man given to studies which helped his prayer life. He learnt to pray according to the word of God and not outside God's word as most Christians are doing today.

The Word of God x-rays our lives and serves as a guide in our relationship with God. The only way we can know how to address issues when we come to God is by studying His word. The word of God is **Spirit and Life** and that was the only thing that silenced the devil when he came to tempt Jesus Christ.

Jesus did not speak on his own accord in confronting the devil. He spoke the word of God. Daniel was able to deliver the children of Israel from captivity because through studying God's word, he found out that they had passed their time of captivity, therefore, he tabled the matter to God through prayers and salvation came.

However, strange unbiblical prayer books are being patronised by Christians who are so shallow in the knowledge of God. They also patronise unbiblical prayer centres which adds up to their problems because they are not based on the word of God.

God says He honours His word above His names – **Psalm 136 v 2.** Whatever name you use in praising and calling God, He honours His word above them all and because He honours His word the devil must bow to the word of God in your life. Amen!

> *"So shall my word be that goeth forth out of my mouth: it shall not return unto me void, but it shall accomplish that which I please, and it shall prosper in the thing whereto I sent it" (Isaiah 55 v 11 – KJV).*

Daniel's conspirators knew that his prayer life was the only way they could trap him. They were so certain that he would fall into their trap; that was why with so much confidence they ensured that the decree was signed by the King.

Daniel was redeemed and heard by God as a result of his righteousness and his fervent prayer life. Since the prayer of a sinner is an abomination to God, the effectual fervent prayer of a righteous man is a delight to God, which availeth much - **James 5 v16, Proverbs 15 v 8.** It was what moved God concerning Daniel. God can only answer you when you pray in righteousness.

CHAPTER 7

The Lion In You

Lions are regarded as wild animals living in a **Pride**. They are the biggest cats in the jungle. A Lion is referred to as the King of the Jungle. Lions have their own community and they do not mingle with other animals in the jungle. It is amazing when we think of Daniel's experience in the lion's den. In those days lions were captured from their prides in the jungle and kept in dens for entertainment and capital punishments.

Having lions was part of the royal status of Kings in the early days as they were used to entertain important guests and their subjects. Also they were used as death penalties for prisoners and state offenders. **'*Damnatio Ad Bestias*'** is the Latin word for - condemnation to beasts. It was a form of the Babylonian capital punishment where condemned persons were killed by lions. That was the situation in which Daniel found himself.

In the early histories of the Roman Empire, the coliseum which could seat 45,000 spectators was home to various gladiatorial battles especially fights between men and beasts including lions, and the killing of Christians by lions was exciting to the Romans to watch. The use of lions for destruction is typical to the description of the devil as a roaring lion looking for who to devour.

However, the God of Daniel is referred to as *'The Lion of the Tribe of Judah'*. There are many characteristics of the lion that portrays the personality of God and His relationship with His children. God expects every one of us to possess such personalities as a lion cannot give birth to a goat but a lion.

Five Lion Characteristics Of God You Must Possess

1. Kingship – God is the King of Kings, and the Lord of Lords – ***Revelation 19 v 16***. He reigns over the heavens and the earth. He installs earthly Kings and dethrones them. In ***Psalm 47 v 7*** He is referred to as the King of all the earth.

In the animal kingdom, the lion is referred to as the *King of the Jungle*. No animal dares come near a lion's pride or toils with a lion. Every other animal maintains their distance from the lion.

Therefore on earth, God has given man dominion as Kings to reign over all the earth – *Genesis 1 v 28*, which man lost after his fall. God did not want to leave man in that fallen state; therefore, He sent the Lord Jesus Christ to reinstall man through his death as King, a royal priesthood and a holy nation – *1st Peter 2 v 9*

We need to understand our royal status. The time is now to exercise our royalty and trample on every other authority that has dominion over us. God has given us a name in the heavens and the earth that will honour our authority as Kings which is the name of Jesus. The authority to rule as Kings on earth was the last rights Jesus gave us when He left the earth. Therefore awake and rise up to your royal estate in Jesus name.

2. Leadership – God right from the time of Abraham has led Israel and taken full responsibility over their affairs. Even when Kings were installed, they enquired from God daily on how to lead the people and God gave directions according to His will. Anything outside this was disastrous to the people even in war times, God gave directions.

God laid down the customs and the way of life of His people which as Christians we must follow because He is our leader. Solomon gave God His rightful place in leadership and God blessed him. Through God's leadership, God taught us how to lead in a godly and selfless manner. As a leader, God sacrificed His only Son to gain the entirety of mankind; therefore he taught us the importance of sacrifice as leaders.

The Lion leads his pride. He is seen as a protector of his pride. Security is guaranteed for the lionesses and the cubs when the lion is around. He safeguards his pride from intruders. The leadership quality of a lion cannot be equaled in comparison to other animals in the jungle. As a leader, he does not eat an entire prey; he leaves some for other animals in the jungle to share in when he is done. He is not selfish.

The lion sleeps for an approximate of 20 hours in a day. The male lion defends the pride while the females are great hunters. Despite the fact that the lion sleeps for long hours, it does not go hungry.

In the beginning after creation, God rested on the seventh day and delegated responsibilities to man. Today man works tirelessly and mostly end up with terminal sicknesses or premature death. This is far from the order God laid down. We are expected to delegate responsibilities, and rest well because we are not slaves just like the lion; but leaders, so that even while we are resting, nothing is grounded.

Most ministers are dying early because they run a one man show. When some ministers die, their ministries die along with them because they did not have the *'Lionic'* nature of leadership, which is putting structures in place through delegating responsibilities and sitting back to rest and watch the system they have put a place run.

3. Strength - God is referred to as our strength. We have no strength of our own. There is absolutely nothing we can do without the strength of God. He empowers us to make exploits because in Him is great strength.

> *"I can do all things through Christ which strengtheneth me" (Philippians 4 v 13).*

> *"He giveth power to the faint; and to them that have no might he increaseth strength"Isaiah 40 v 29).*

The lion is the strongest animal in the jungle. His strength cannot be equaled to any animal. He cannot be a weak King. Kingship goes with great strength in order to withstand attacks and adversaries. The strength of the lion makes him King over the jungle.

The reason Satan could not overthrow God is because of the strength of God which makes Him Mighty. David referred to God as his Strength - *Psalm 73 v 26*. The Bible says the only reason we can do all things and be victorious is only through the strength of God – *Isaiah 40 v 31.*

God can strengthen you in your weakness. Therefore do not hesitate to call on him for strength when things are hard on you or when you cannot go on any longer. He is there to strengthen you. Study the word of God in order to have and exercise your strength which is embedded in God's word because a weak Christian can never be victorious.

God has given us the ability, wisdom, strength, power and might to do all things because He has already strengthened us.

4. Boldness – The boldness of God qualifies him as the Lion of the tribe of Judah. You cannot approach God if you are not bold. The death of Jesus Christ tore the veil of the Holy of Holies into two so that we can come before God in boldness.

The Bible says that God has not given us the Spirit of fear but the Spirit of boldness and of a sound mind -*2 Timothy 1 v 7.* Praise God! There is no way you can be sound if you have the Spirit of fear. A fearful person is a confused person. God wants to see your boldness in confronting challenges and the powers of darkness because it is only through your boldness that you can exercise the authority God has given you.

The Lion is so bold that nothing scares him. In fact he is a dread to every animal in the jungle. No human being can withstand a lion. Humans also dread it. God wants us to be a dread to forces that are bent on disgracing our Kingship. Praise the Lord!

> "This very day, I will begin to put the dread of thee and fear of thee upon the nations that are under the whole heaven, who shall hear report of thee, and shall tremble, and be in anguish because of thee" (Deuteronomy 2 v 25).

5. Fierceness – God does not tolerate any thing that is evil. He is fiercely angry against evil. His fierceness is exhibited in his hunting power to hunt down anything that opposes His will. He hunted down Satan and his allies from heaven to the earth and created a fierce place for their judgment – Hell.

God's fierceness is exhibited in His name. He is referred to as a **Consuming Fire** and **'The Terrible God' – Deuteronomy 4 v24, Hebrews 12 v 29**. His fire is so fierce that nothing can stand in its way. God wants us to have that fierce nature against evil.

> "For the Lord Most High is terrible; he is a great King over all the earth" (Psalm 42 v 12).

God is fierce in battle. He does not spare what should not be spared. He is referred to as the **'Man of War' – Exodus 15 v 3**. He told us categorically not to avenge for ourselves because He alone has the tact in vengeance and battles.

We can only have this nature which is imminent in a Lion if we study the word of God and spend quality time in his presence. God wants us to be battle ready at all times. The Bible says we should be vigilant because we have an adversary going about as a roaring lion looking for whom to devour – *1st Peter 5 v 8.*

The Lion is always at alert. He is battle ready even when asleep. He cannot be taken unawares, neither can he be conquered. Your skills in battle can only be sharpened on the word of God. You must be battle ready in order to maintain the status of being more than a conqueror – **Romans 8 v 37.**

One reason I believe the Lions in the den could not harm Daniel is because they saw a boldness in Daniel that defiled their boldness and they knew that someone more fierce had entered their den. I believe they were so glad when Daniel left their den as the sight of him was enough scare for them which made them too timid to harm him. Halleluyah!

Even animals reverence those who know their God, for they shall do exploits as recorded concerning Daniel. Therefore take your place as a lion in destiny and dominate in Jesus name.

Prayer Points To Shut The Lions Mouth

The God of Daniel is the one that has the final say. He alone can upturn negative judgements and set the captive free.

- He will set you free in Jesus name.

- Any conspiracy against you will fail in Jesus name.

- Remain steadfastness.

- Remain Righteous.

- Remain Holy.

- Remain faithful to your God.

- Remain prayerful.

And the God of Daniel will strengthen you to shut the lion's mouth, in the name of Jesus. Amen.

PRAYER

In the name of Jesus Christ

*God I thank you for revealing to me how to shut
the mouths of the lions in my life.*

*Father in your mercy grant me the gift of faith
to shut every lion roaring against my destiny.*

*I stand against powers working against
righteousness in my life. I terminate their
assignment over my destiny.*

*I decree that the time is up for every wandering
spirit making me unstable in my service to God. I receive
strength to be steadfast in my service to God.*

*Oh Lord my Father by your mercy empower me in
the place of prayer. Let the anointing of ceaseless and
effectual prayers fall upon me.*

*I receive boldness to trample upon every lion
working against my glory.*

Father cause the mantle of leadership to rest upon me so that I can manifest in your blessings, to rule, and dominate.

Thank you Father because I know you have heard and answered me.

Shut The Lion's Mouth

Bible Quotations That Will Bring Out The Lion In You

FAITH

"So then faith cometh by hearing, and hearing by the word of God" (Romans 10 v 17).

"But without faith it is impossible to pleases him: for he that cometh to God must believe that he is, and that he is a rewarder of them that diligently seek him" (Hebrews 11 v 6).

"And Jesus answering saith unto them, Have faith in God" (Mark 11 v 22).

"For by grace are ye saved through faith; and that not of yourselves: it is the gift of God" (Ephesians 2 v 8).

"That your faith should not stand in the wisdom of men, but in the power of God"(1 Corinthians 2 v 5).

RIGHTEOUSNESS

"Blessed are they that keep judgement, and he that doeth righteousness at all times" (Psalm 106 v 3).

"For I say unto you, That except your righteousness shall exceed the righteousness of the scribes and Pharisees, ye shall in no case enter the kingdom of heaven" (Mathew 5 v 20).

"Flee also youthful lusts: but follow righteousness, faith, charity, peace, with them that call on the Lord out of a pure heart" (2 Timothy 2 v 22).

"Being filled with the fruits of righteousness, which are by Jesus Christ, unto the glory and praise of God" (Philippians 1 v 11).

"But and if ye suffer for righteousness' sake, happy are ye: and be not afraid of their terror, neither be troubled" (1 Peter 3 v 14).

STEADFASTNESS

"Therefore, my beloved brethren, be ye steadfast, unmovable, always abounding in the work of the Lord, forasmuch as ye know that your labour is not in vain in the Lord" (1st Corinthians 15 v 58).

"But they that wait upon the LORD shall renew their strength; they shall mount up with wings as eagles; they shall run, and not be weary; and they shall walk and not faint" (Isaiah 40 v 31).

"He shall not be afraid of evil tidings: his heart is fixed trusting in the Lord" (Psalm 112 v 7).

"Blessed is the man that endureth temptation: for when he is tried, he shall receive the crown of life, which the Lord hath promised to them that love him"(James 1 v 12).

"That by two immutable things, in which it was impossible for God to lie, we might have a strong consolation, who have fled for refuge to lay hold upon the hope set before us" (Hebrews 6 v 18).

PRAYER

"And pray in the spirit on all occasions with all kinds of prayers and requests. With this in mind, be alert and always keep on praying for all the Lord's people" (Ephesians 6 v 18).

"Rejoice evermore. Pray without ceasing. In everything give thanks: for this is the will of God in Christ Jesus concerning you"(1 Thessalonian 5 v 16 – 18).

"Continue in prayer, and watch in the same with thanksgiving"
(Colossians 4 v2).

"Then shall you call upon me, and ye shall go and pray unto me,
and I will hearken unto you" (Jeremiah 29 v 12).

"Rejoicing in hope; patient in tribulation; continuing instant in
prayer' (Romans 12 v 12).

"Call unto me, and I will answer thee, and show the great and
mighty things, which thou knowest not" (Jeremiah 33 v 3).

DELIVERANCE FROM CONSPIRACY

"For they intended evil against thee: they imagined a mischievous
device, which they are not able to perform" (Psalm 21 v 11).

"Woe to them that devise iniquity, and work evil upon their
beds!(Micah 2 v 1).

"He disappointeth the devices of the crafty, so that their hands
cannot perform their enterprise"(Job 5 v 12).

"Arise, O LORD; Punish the wicked, O God! Do not ignore the
helpless" (Psalm 10 v 2 – NLT).

"The Lord shall fight for you, and ye shall hold your peace" (Exodus 14 v 14).